the church CLIP ART book

the church CLIP ART book

Illustrations, headlines and borders
for creative church bulletins,
calendars, and newsletters.

Written and Illustrated by
Steve Hunt and Dave Adamson

ZondervanPublishingHouse
Grand Rapids, Michigan

A Division of HarperCollinsPublishers

THE CHURCH CLIP ART BOOK
Copyright © 1988 by Steve Hunt and Dave Adamson of The Church Art Works™

Requests for information should be addressed to:
Zondervan Publishing House
Grand Rapids, Michigan 49530

Library of Congress Cataloging in Publication Data

Hunt, Steve.
    The church clip art book / written and illustrated, Steve Hunt and Dave Adamson.
        p.   cm.
    "Ministry resources library."
    ISBN 0-310-31591-3
    1. Church bulletins. I. Adamson, Dave. II. Title.
BV653.3.H86   1988
246—dc19   87-30270
                                                                             CIP

Printed in the United States of America

95 96 97 98 99 00 01 02 / CH / 16 15 14 13 12 11 10 9

C·O·N·T·E·N·T·S

I·N·T·R·O·D·U·C·T·I·O·N

This helpful book will lead you in an adventure that is both fun and rewarding as you communicate with your church. It will assist you in generating excitement about the activities and programs you regularly promote.

For those unfamiliar with "clip art" and how it is used, we will give an overview of its purpose.

Clip art is a collection of general-interest artwork that can be used to illustrate an announcement or church bulletin or newsletter. All you have to do is plan your copy, choose the piece of art that best illustrates what you have to say, and assemble the master paste-up sheet that is to be duplicated.

Whether you are from a small church or a large one, a rural congregation or an urban ministry, there is a common need to communicate well. Sometimes written communication can be as simple as the Sunday church bulletin or as diversified as an eight-page weekly newsletter published in two or three colors. Sometimes the product can be accomplished by a church secretary alone, or it may involve several people working together.

Probably the most visible church publication is the Sunday worship folder or "bulletin." Sometimes these are combined into one, containing both an order of service and the announcement of activities. In other cases there are two publications—a folder that relates only to worship and the order of service, and a newsletter or folder that contains a variety of announcements and information.

Whichever format you choose, a bulletin can become highly interesting with a little extra effort. Instead of using your church name on the cover—people seated in the sanctuary usually know what church they're in—use a beautiful calligraphy verse or inspiring phrase to challenge their hearts.

Inside the bulletin, use borders and sport illustrations to add interest. Bold title "bars" for headings like TODAY or TONIGHT or MIDWEEK help break up the monotony of type.

Secretaries find that the church newsletter can be a great place to use clip art. Depending on the way it's folded, the newsletter can have one or two or three columns. By varying the columns, a myriad of eye-catching layouts can be used to include clip art or borders.

Pastors can use clip art in study notes handed out at a midweek service. Instead of a typed outline only, begin the page with an illustration. It changes a plain sheet of notes into a visually interesting and thought-provoking piece.

Another use pastors find for clip art is in preparing transparencies for overhead projectors. Overheads are a great place to use a punchy heading like CELEBRATE when studying the Resurrection, or DON'T MISS IT when emphasizing an important point. The degree of success will largely depend on just how creative you are in choosing the art.

In the Christian education department, clip art can be used to make bulletin boards more attractive than ever. The art can be enlarged with an opaque projector and traced to make large illustrations. Add some color to make them bright and eye-catching.

The same technique can be used for making large signs, banners, or posters for special events. In making banners, you may have to enlarge your clip art on a photocopier before putting it on the opaque projector. If you don't have an opaque projector, take a picture of the clip art with "Kodalith" 35mm film, then project the image with an ordinary slide projector. These large blowups are great for emphasizing a theme. Begin the promotion by using clip art in an announcement piece such as a flyer or handout. Then use it in the printed program distributed at the event and as a large banner behind the speaker's platform.

Youth and camp leaders have many activities that offer uses for clip art. Even T-shirts can be designed to include a great graphic from this book and then combined with the church's name or an event's theme.

Enjoy your opportunity to make your publications more interesting. Like anything else, planning ahead will make your efforts more successful. By editing your copy and allowing space for illustrations, you will be able to bring a lot of interest to your publications and church activities.

—*Steve and Dave*

A·C·K·N·O·W·L·E·D·G·M·E·N·T·S

In 1984 we began developing a subscription clip-art service for churches called The Church Art Works. Our goal was to assist churches with a new contemporary art service that would emphasize bold, energetic illustrations of current themes. We wanted to maintain a high standard of quality to improve the publications that churches produce.

The endeavor was well-received, and our library is ever-expanding. This book is a compilation of the best art from our first three volumes.

We would like to thank our staff for their dedicated work in assisting us in the production of our art. Thank you to our ladies—Kirsten Urbigkeit and Kelley Adamson—and to our guys—Rick Lindemann, John Bolesky, Ken Black, Bruce Bottorff, and Jim O'Halloran—our production staff. Additional thanks to the hundreds of churches that have helped us with ideas and encouragement.

Valentasia — alternate name for a valentines event or banquet.

Valentasia

WATCH NIGHT SERVICE

You're Invited!
NEW YEARS.
GET TOGETHER

Valentines DAY

Valentines DAY

You're Invited!
NEW YEARS.
GET TOGETHER

WATCH NIGHT SERVICE

Valentasia

Palm Sunday

Palm Sunday

A Wedding

Palm Sunday

A Wedding

A Wedding

Pentecost

Pentecost

Pentecost

EASTER

EASTER

EASTER
CANTATA

EASTER
CANTATA

EASTER
CANTATA

GOOD FRIDAY

GOOD FRIDAY

PASSOVER

PASSOVER

M·O·T·H·E·R

FATHERS' Day

FATHERS DAY

FATHERS' Day

M·O·T·H·E·R

FATHERS DAY

M·O·T·H·E·R

MOTHER-DAUGHTER
BANQUET

AMERICA

GOD SHED HIS   GRACE ON THEE

MEMORIAL DAY

MEMORIAL DAY

MEMORIAL DAY

AN OLD FASHIONED HALLOWEEN PARTY

HALLOWEEN PARTY

REFORMATION DAY

HALLOWEEN PARTY

COSTUME PARTY

COSTUME PARTY

ALL SAINTS DAY

AN OLD FASHIONED HALLOWEEN PARTY

ALL SAINTS DAY

THANKSGIVING

THANKSGIVING

CHRIST THE SAVIOR ~IS~ BORN

CHRIST THE SAVIOR ~IS~ BORN

Christmas
CELEBRATION
OF CHRIST'S BIRTH

Christmas
CELEBRATION
OF CHRIST'S BIRTH

Bridal Shower

Bridal Shower

Baby Shower

PRIME TIMERS

Bridal Shower

(Name for Mid-age fellowship group)

PRIME TIMERS

FELLOWSHIP & RECREATION

POTLUCK

MORNING BREAK

A Bible Study for Young Mothers

Women's Bible Study

WHITE ELEPHANT PARTY

POTLUCK

MORNING BREAK
A Bible Study for Young Mothers

Women's Bible Study

Women's Bible Study

POTLUCK

WHITE ELEPHANT PARTY

Home
Bible Study

Home
Bible Study

Home
Bible Study

BABY
Shower

BABY
Shower

BABY
Shower

(Name for twenties'n thirties fellowship group)

Ladies'
Night
Out

BATTER BASH

A Christmas Cookie Making Party

BATTER BASH

A Christmas Cookie Making Party

F·E·L·L·O·W·S·H·I·P

Sunday School

F·E·L·L·O·W·S·H·I·P

F·E·L·L·O·W·S·H·I·P

Sunday School

Sunday School

A SINGLES FELLOWSHIP

(Monthly dinners at a
new restaurant each
month.)

Note: SALT stands for
Single Adults Learning
Together, or any other
name you choose.

Senior Skip Day

Senior Skip Day

Senior Skip Day

HOME MADE
ICE CREAM
PARTY

CHRISTIAN FILM NIGHT

HOME MADE
ICE CREAM
PARTY

CHRISTIAN FILM NIGHT

JOY FELLOWSHIP

JOY FELLOWSHIP

Afterglow

JOY FELLOWSHIP

Afterglow

WESTERN NITE

WESTERN NITE

Afterglow

Where in the world is God working?

Oh give thanks to the LORD for He is good!

Oh give thanks to the LORD for He is good!

Come let us Worship

Oh give thanks to the LORD for He is good!

Come let us Worship

Where in the world is God working?

Come let us Worship

Where in the world is God working?

Praise the Lord!

Praise the Lord!

Praise the Lord!

Casting
ALL
YOUR CARE
UPON HIM
FOR HE
CARES
FOR YOU.

Sing unto the Lord a new Song!

Casting
ALL
YOUR CARE
UPON HIM
FOR HE
CARES
FOR YOU.

Casting
ALL
YOUR CARE
UPON HIM
FOR HE
CARES
FOR YOU.

Sing unto the Lord a new Song!

Sing unto the Lord a new Song!

What a difference you're made in my life!

What a difference you're made in my life!

What a difference you're made in my life!

El Shaddai
The All-Sufficient One

El Shaddai
The All-Sufficient One

CELEBRATE
The Life of God

El Shaddai
The All-Sufficient One

CARE
About One Another in Christ

CULTIVATE
Personal Growth in Christ

COMMUNICATE
Christ To Our World

CELEBRATE
The Life of God

CARE
About One Another in Christ

CULTIVATE
Personal Growth in Christ

COMMUNICATE
Christ To Our World

CELEBRATE
The Life of God

CARE
About One Another in Christ

CULTIVATE
Personal Growth in Christ

COMMUNICATE
Christ To Our World

REJOICE!

Rejoice!

God With Us
Immanuel

You Are
the Light
of the
World

God
With Us
Immanuel

REJOICE!
Rejoice!

God With Us
Immanuel

REJOICE!
Rejoice!

You Are
the Light
of the
World

You Are
the Light
of the
World

Called to Excellence

Called to Excellence

I WILL
LIFT UP MY EYES
UNTO THE [hills icon] HILLS FROM
WHENCE [icon] COMETH
MY STRENGTH

I WILL
LIFT UP MY EYES
UNTO THE [hills icon] HILLS FROM
WHENCE [icon] COMETH
MY STRENGTH

Called to Excellence

I WILL
LIFT UP MY EYES
UNTO THE [hills icon] HILLS FROM
WHENCE [icon] COMETH
MY STRENGTH

Rejoice, and again I say— Rejoice!

Rejoice, and again I say— Rejoice!

Rejoice, and again I say— Rejoice!

THOU
ART WORTHY
O LORD, TO
RECEIVE GLORY,
HONOR &
PRAISE.&

THOU
ART WORTHY
O LORD, TO
RECEIVE GLORY,
HONOR &
PRAISE.&

I am
the Bread
of Life

THOU
ART WORTHY
O LORD, TO
RECEIVE GLORY,
HONOR &
PRAISE.&

WE
EXALT
THEE, O
LORD

WE
EXALT
THEE, O
LORD

I am
the Bread
of Life

WE
EXALT
THEE, O
LORD

BE STRONG AND OF GOOD COURAGE.

BE STRONG AND OF GOOD COURAGE.

BE STRONG AND OF GOOD COURAGE.

Praise the Lord Oh my Soul!

HEAVEN
AND EARTH SHALL
PASS AWAY, BUT
MY WORDS SHALL
NOT PASS AWAY.

Praise the Lord Oh my Soul!

HEAVEN
AND EARTH SHALL
PASS AWAY,
MY WORDS SHALL
NOT PASS AWAY.

HEAVEN
AND EARTH SHALL
PASS AWAY, BUT
MY WORDS SHALL
NOT PASS AWAY.

Praise the Lord Oh my Soul!

Thou wilt keep him in perfect peace whose mind is stayed on Thee.

ISAIAH 26:3

O Lord, how majestic is your name in all the earth.

Thou wilt keep him in perfect peace whose mind is stayed on Thee.

ISAIAH 26:3

Thou wilt keep him in perfect peace whose mind is stayed on Thee.

ISAIAH 26:3

O Lord, how majestic is your name in all the earth.

Hallelujah!

Hallelujah!

Hallelujah!

O Lord, how majestic is your name in all the earth.

Follow me as I follow Christ

Follow me as I follow Christ

OUR GOD REIGNS

COME CELEBRATE JESUS!

COME CELEBRATE JESUS!

COME CELEBRATE JESUS!

OUR GOD REIGNS

OUR GOD REIGNS

Follow me as I follow Christ

PEOPLE — AGE GROUPS

BAPTISM

ENCOURAGING

PRAISE

BIBLE STUDY

SERVICE

PRAISE

ENCOURAGING

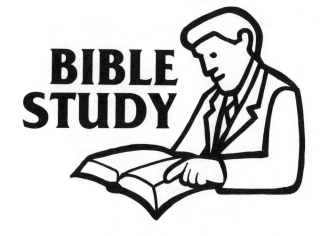

BIBLE STUDY

SERVICE

SPIRITUAL EMPHASIS

THY WORD IS SHARPER THAN ANY TWO-EDGED SWORD

THY WORD IS SHARPER THAN ANY TWO-EDGED SWORD

STRENGTH IN THE FACE OF TESTING
JOB

STRENGTH IN THE FACE OF TESTING
JOB

THY WORD IS SHARPER THAN ANY TWO-EDGED SWORD

STRENGTH IN THE FACE OF TESTING
JOB

KNOWING *God's Will*

MEMO
Be Faithful
Love one Another
Be Joyful
Hate Sin
Peacemaker

KNOWING *God's Will*

FOR
GOD
SO LOVED
THE
WORLD THAT HE
GAVE HIS ONLY
BEGOTTEN SON
THAT WHOSOEVER
BELIEVETH IN HIM
SHOULD NOT PERISH
BUT HAVE
EVERLASTING
LIFE.

FOR
GOD
SO LOVED
THE
WORLD THAT HE
GAVE HIS ONLY
BEGOTTEN SON
THAT WHOSOEVER
BELIEVETH IN HIM
SHOULD NOT PERISH
BUT HAVE
EVERLASTING
LIFE.

FOR
GOD
SO LOVED
THE
WORLD THAT HE
GAVE HIS ONLY
BEGOTTEN SON
THAT WHOSOEVER
BELIEVETH IN HIM
SHOULD NOT PERISH
BUT HAVE
EVERLASTING
LIFE.

The HOME

MEMO
Be Faithful
Love one Another
Be Joyful
Hate Sin
Peacemaker

KNOWING *God's Will*

The HOME

The HOME

SPIRITUAL GIFTS

JOIN US WEDNESDAY FOR
SHARING & BIBLE STUDY

DIVORCE
RECOVERY PROGRAM

SPIRITUAL GIFTS

SPIRITUAL GIFTS

DIVORCE
RECOVERY PROGRAM

JOIN US WEDNESDAY FOR
SHARING & BIBLE STUDY

JOIN US WEDNESDAY FOR
SHARING & BIBLE STUDY

ALL FOR THE ASKING
Studies on Prayer

old Testament Journeys

BREAKING HABITUAL SIN

old Testament Journeys

ALL FOR THE ASKING
Studies on Prayer

ALL FOR THE ASKING
Studies on Prayer

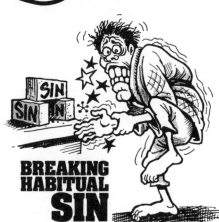

BREAKING HABITUAL SIN

BREAKING HABITUAL SIN

KNIT TOGETHER IN LOVE

THE OTHER HALF

THE OTHER HALF

THE OTHER HALF

KNIT TOGETHER IN LOVE

KNIT TOGETHER IN LOVE

Knock
and it shall
be opened
unto you

The Ministry of
PAUL

The Ministry of
PAUL

Knock
and it shall
be opened
unto you

The Ministry of
PAUL

STUDIES IN
A·C·T·S
THE CHURCH IS BORN

STUDIES IN
A·C·T·S
THE CHURCH IS BORN

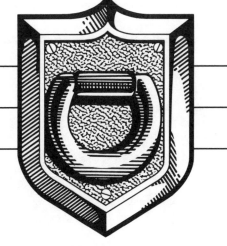
Knock
and it shall
be opened
unto you

STUDIES IN
A·C·T·S
THE CHURCH IS BORN

LIBRARY

LIBRARY

WOMEN'S MINISTRIES

WOMEN'S MINISTRIES

OUT~REACH

OUT~REACH

LIBRARY

OUTREACH

OUT~REACH

WOMEN'S MINISTRIES

OUTREACH

Big Buddy

PIE
SOCIAL

Big Buddy

PIE
SOCIAL

POWER HOUR

PIE
SOCIAL

Big Buddy

POWER HOUR

POWER HOUR

Youth MINISTRIES

Couples MINISTRIES

Sr. Adult MINISTRIES

Family MINISTRIES

Singles MINISTRIES

Adult MINISTRIES

Children's MINISTRIES

Shut-in MINISTRIES

Care Closet

PASTOR'S CORNER

Sunday School

Care Closet

Sunday School

Sunday School

PASTOR'S CORNER

Care Closet

PASTOR'S CORNER

We Need
YOU
in Teacher
Training!

We Need
YOU
in Teacher
Training!

We Need
YOU
in Teacher
Training!

BABY
DEDICATION

BABY
DEDICATION

BABY
DEDICATION

BABY
DEDICATION

Infant Baptism

Infant Baptism

Infant Baptism

WORKDAY
AT THE CHURCH

WORKDAY
AT THE CHURCH

WORKDAY
AT THE CHURCH

We're Growing!

We're Growing!

We're Growing!

This Week's Message

This Week's Message

This Week's Message

EUROPE

EUROPE

SOUTH AMERICA

EUROPE

SOUTH AMERICA

EUROPE

SOUTH AMERICA

DEACONS MEETING

DEACONS MEETING

DEACONS MEETING

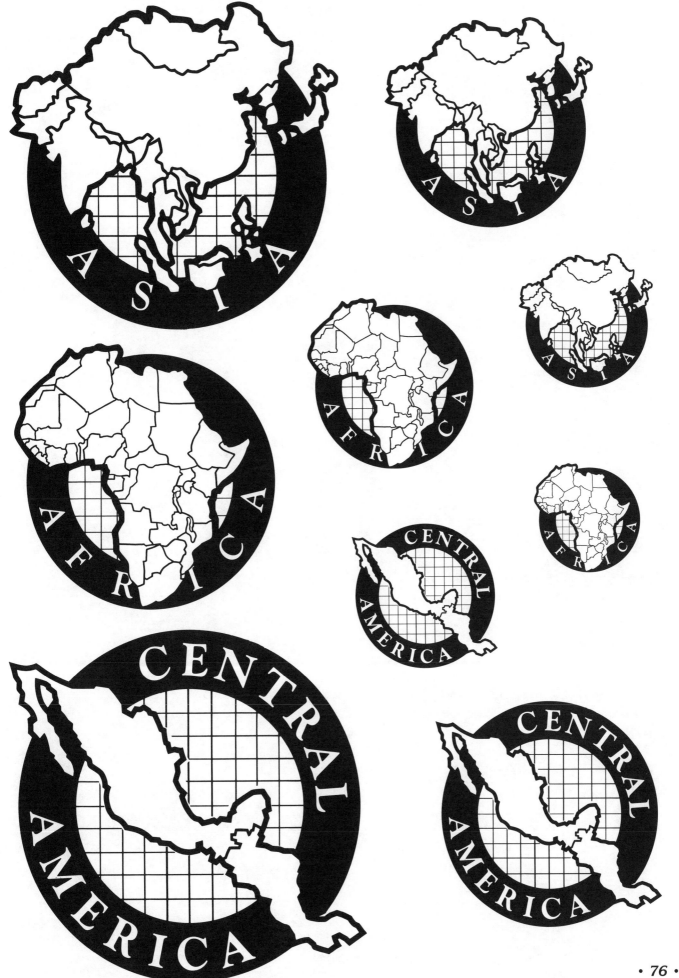

Congratulations!

Congratulations!

BRING YOUR BIBLE and a FRIEND!

BRING YOUR BIBLE and a FRIEND!

Congratulations!

BRING YOUR BIBLE and a FRIEND!

MISSIONS
WHITE UNTO HARVEST

Congratulations!

MISSIONS
WHITE UNTO HARVEST

BRING YOUR BIBLE and a FRIEND!

MISSIONS
WHITE UNTO HARVEST

LOOKING AHEAD

 LOOKING AHEAD

 LOOKING AHEAD

 Baptismal Service

Baptismal Service

 Baptismal Service

Agenda:
1. Prayer
2. Annual Budget
3. Election

Business Meeting

Agenda:
1. Prayer
2. Annual Budget
3. Election

 **Business Meeting**

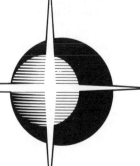

DOES THE THOUGHT OF **SERVICE** MAKE YOU **NERVOUS?**

LIFESTYLE EVANGELISM

DOES THE THOUGHT OF **SERVICE** MAKE YOU **NERVOUS?**

LIFESTYLE EVANGELISM

LIFESTYLE EVANGELISM

DOES THE THOUGHT OF **SERVICE** MAKE YOU **NERVOUS?**

MISSIONS
PLANTING SEEDS OF FAITH WORLDWIDE

MISSIONS
PLANTING SEEDS OF FAITH WORLDWIDE

MISSIONS
PLANTING SEEDS OF FAITH WORLDWIDE

All the King's Men

All the King's Men

SOLO WALK

Visit the LIBRARY
GREAT CHRISTIAN HEROES

Visit the LIBRARY
GREAT CHRISTIAN HEROES

SOLO WALK

SOLO WALK

Visit the LIBRARY
GREAT CHRISTIAN HEROES

Aerobics Class

Aerobics Class

Aerobics Class

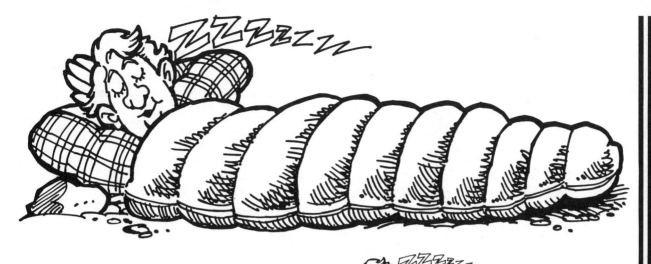

MEN'S GETAWAY

MEN'S RETREAT

MEN'S RETREAT

MEN'S RETREAT

WOMEN'S RETREAT

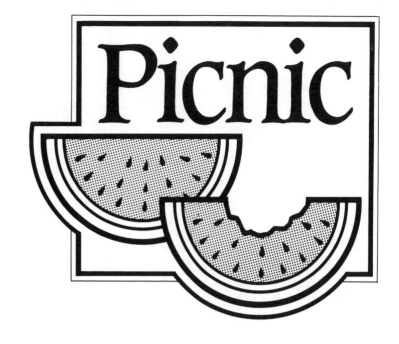

Picnic

Come Along!
WINTER
RETREAT

Come Along!
WINTER
RETREAT

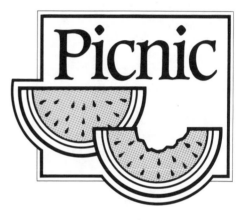

Picnic

Come Along!
WINTER
RETREAT

WOMEN'S RETREAT

Picnic

WOMEN'S RETREAT

DayCamp

RV CAMPOUT

DayCamp

FLAG FOOTBALL

RV CAMPOUT

RV CAMPOUT

FLAG FOOTBALL

DayCamp

WE NEED CAMP COUNSELORS!

WE NEED CAMP
COUNSELORS!

SUMMER CAMP'S COMING!

WE NEED CAMP COUNSELORS!

SUMMER CAMP'S COMING!

SUMMER CAMP'S COMING!

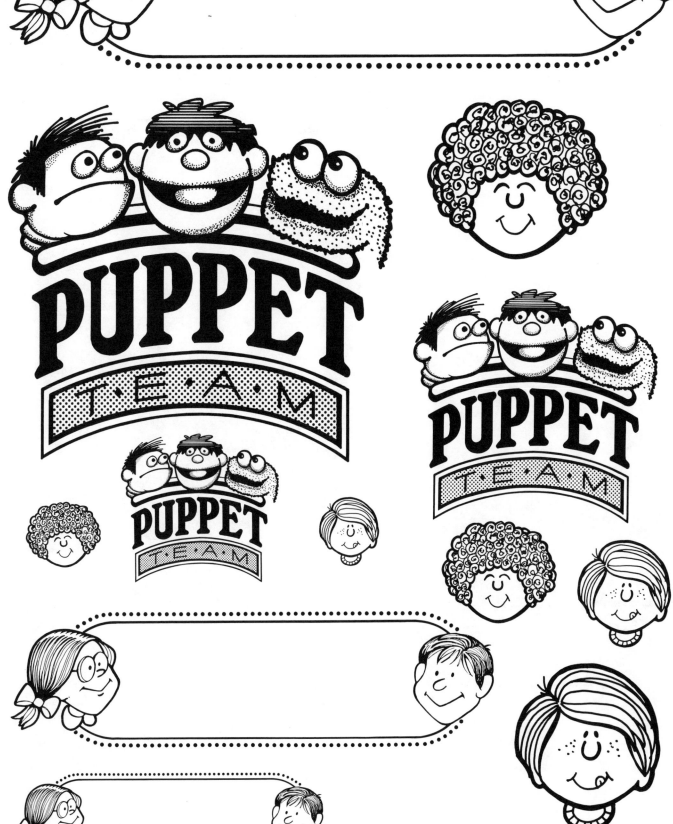

CHILDREN'S CHURCH

CHILDREN'S CHURCH

CHILDREN'S CHURCH

NURSERY CARE

NURSERY CARE

NURSERY CARE

We're learning about NOAH

We're learning about DANIEL

We're learning about DANIEL

We're learning about DANIEL

We're learning about DANIEL

We're learning about NOAH

We're learning about NOAH

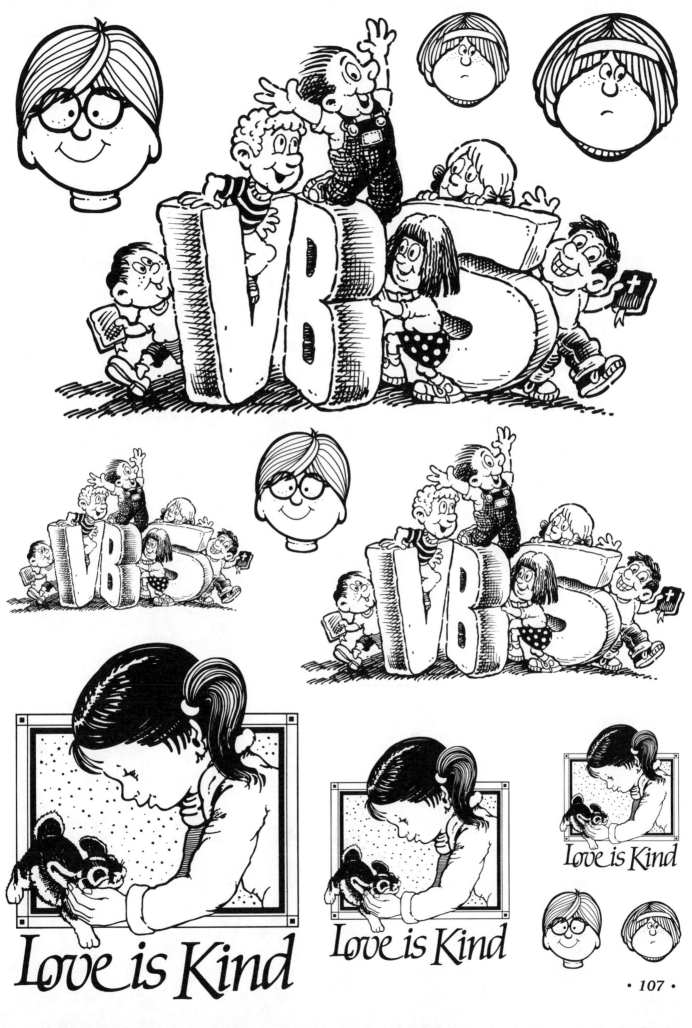

MUSIC NOTES

MUSIC NOTES

MUSIC NOTES

An Evening of Singing

An Evening of Singing

An Evening of Singing

Christian Musical

DRAMA

Christian Musical

DRAMA

Christian Musical

DRAMA

SUNDAY NIGHT

Sing!

SUNDAY NIGHT

Sing!

SUNDAY NIGHT

Sing!

Now's the time to join the Choir!

Now's the time to join the Choir!

Now's the time to join the Choir!

Sing unto the Lord a new Song!

Sing unto the Lord a new Song!

Sing unto the Lord a new Song!

NEWSLETTER

Space for Name, Dates, etc.

WEDNESDAY

SPECIAL ACTIVITIES

SPECIAL OPPORTUNITIES

FROM THE PASTOR

NOTES

TODAY

THIS WEEK

COMING NEXT SUNDAY

WORSHIP SERVICE

EVENING SERVICE

The Heavens Declare the Glory of God

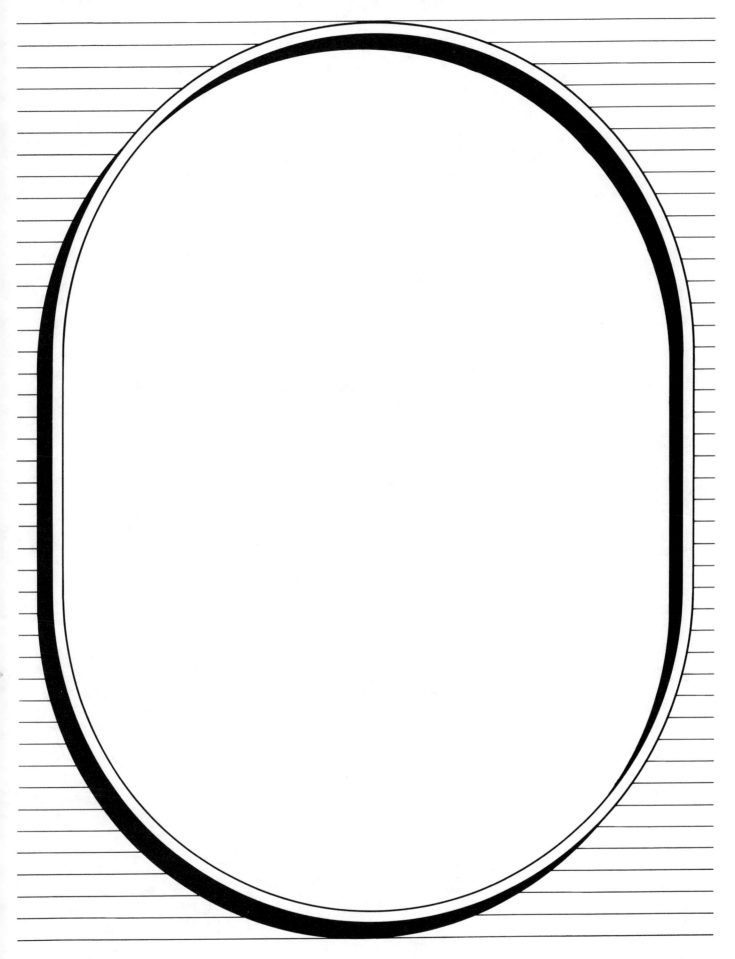

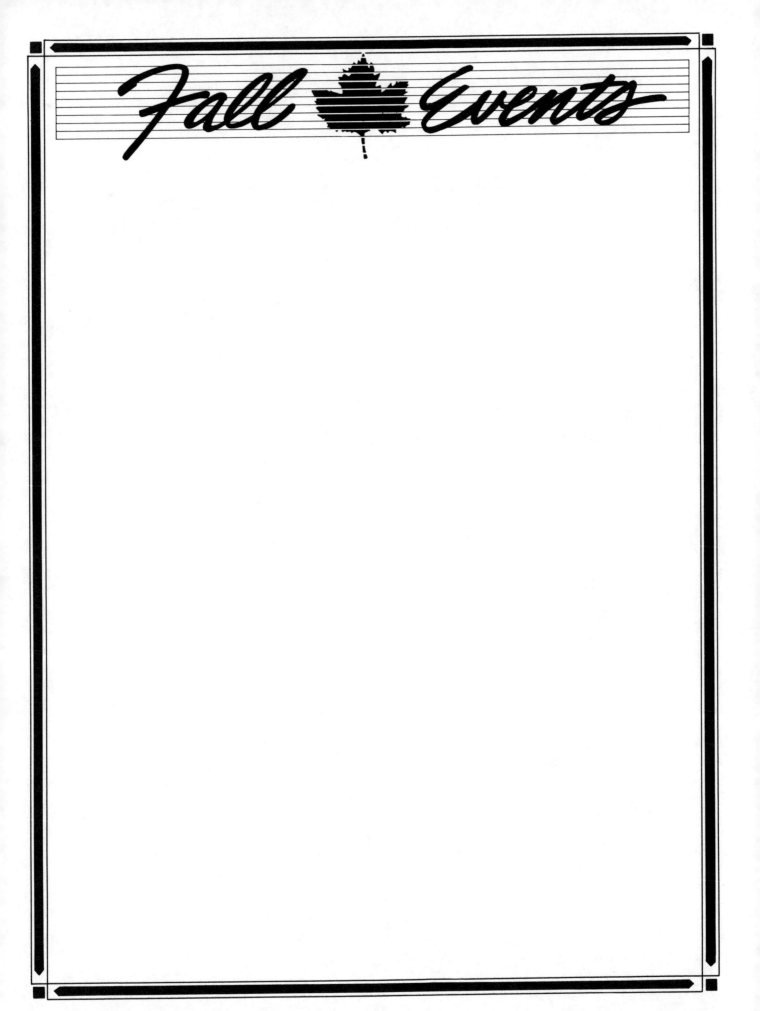

Fall Events

Thanksgiving

GOD BLESS
AMERICA

EASTER

J·A·N·U·A·R·Y

F·E·B·R·U·A·R·Y

M·A·R·C·H

A·P·R·I·L

M·A·Y

J·U·N·E

J·U·L·Y

A·U·G·U·S·T

S·E·P·T·E·M·B·E·R

O·C·T·O·B·E·R

N·O·V·E·M·B·E·R

D·E·C·E·M·B·E·R

1·9·9·0

1·9·8·9

1·9·8·8

JULY

AUGUST

SEPTEMBER

OCTOBER

NOVEMBER

DECEMBER

JANUARY

FEBRUARY

MARCH

APRIL

MAY

JUNE

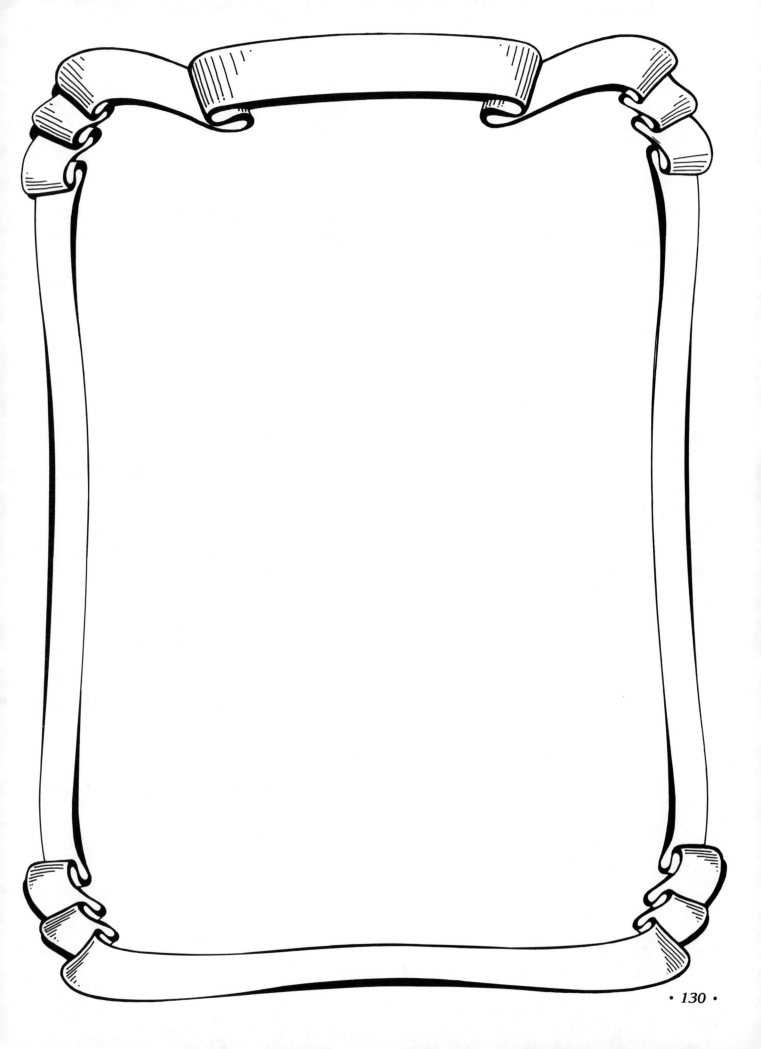

I·N·D·E·X